# More

# Men

# Cracked

# Open

British Library Cataloguing in Publication Data:

a catalogue record for this publication

is available from the British Library

ISBN   978-1-912052-55-4

© Handsel Press for *The Male Journey* 2020

The right of editor Robert Davison to be identified as 'the author' of this work on behalf of *The Male Journey* has been asserted by him in accordance with the Copyright, Designs and Patents Act 1988

Typeset in 11.5pt Calibri at Haddington, Scotland

Printed by West Port Print & Design, St Andrews

Cover Design by Simon Ray

*The Male Journey* is a registered Charity 1163767

# Introduction

In this second collection of poetry from The Male Journey, men once again delve deep and share their personal sore spots, vulnerabilities and intensely personal reflections on life; the kind of revelations that are usually kept hidden away.

While there are a handful of lighter verses, most draw from a deeper, darker place. The reason being that through their search for inner peace and wholeness, many have encountered the paradox that on the other side of personal darkness awaits light; that squarely facing pain, guilt or shame brings relief; and that the act of admitting to vulnerability can be the gateway to uncovering totally unexpected strengths.

Here's an analogy. To bring a sliding car under control and prevent a catastrophe, instructors teach "stay off the brakes and turn into the skid". These two actions, especially under conditions of stress or fear are the precise opposite of most people's instinctive reaction. This is not so different from our instinctive response in life when disturbing thoughts or unbearable emotions threaten to send us spinning out of control towards a different kind of catastrophe – it's easy to put the brakes on and turn away! So, when life becomes slippery, dare we stay off the brakes and take courage to turn towards our most difficult thoughts or feelings? Many men find this hard, even terrifying. But paradoxically, by "turning towards", we will often experience a breakthrough moment, where we find ourselves guided to discover what become some of our most reassuring and treasured stepping-stones for life. Thanks to the courage and generosity of our contributors, this poetry illuminates many ways of turning into the skid.

I hope you find points of connection in this material, drawn from the everyday life of men who have undertaken our Rites of Passage or participated in our regular group meetings (usually outdoors in nature, around a fire). If you are curious about these Rites, the collection will provide a glimpse of the territory. You can also visit our website. In any case, may these poems inspire or remind you to keep turning into life's skids.

Robert Davison
Editor
on behalf of The Male Journey
www.malejourney.org.uk

# Contents

## Peace

Posture of openness

Emptying of our hearts

Allowing space for the Divine

Conceding that we are not in control

Embracing mystery

Peace – be calm and accept all that is, all that has been, and all that will be.

Peace – so desperately sought for and yet so hard to attain.

Peace – know in the furthest depths of my heart that I will get through this even though everything within screams I cannot.

Peace – take the agonising choice to forgive when my body still trembles at the memories of how I was wronged.

Peace – accept that life is hard but will make me grow.

Peace – know that I am not the only important thing in this world, and know what *is*.

Peace – concede that I am not in full control and trust the process of refinement that life is taking me through.

Peace – accept that physical death is not the end, but the beginning.

*Judah Chandra*

## To My Dad

Dad, I miss you.
I get angry and think of how I could have changed things. Helped you.
O what pain you must have been in and what torment.
My anger these years has shrouded my vision; preventing me from
    understanding what you must have gone through.
All that responsibility and expectation on your shoulders with no one to
    talk to.

I think of you and what could have been:
    placing my small hands against yours to feel the grooves of your palms
        and tracing my fingers across them,
    welcoming me home after a long travel,
    guiding me and laughing with me during those teenage years of angst,
    receiving your strong protective embrace when I felt useless and
        overwhelmed,
    hearing your majestic belly laugh,
    ruffling your beard and feeling the heat of your skin on my hands,
    wrapping my arms around you and feeling the strength of your sinews
        beneath,
    smiling at me with pride at my graduation,
    meeting my future wife and mischievously asking her questions at your
        first encounter,
    being there for my child's first birthday.

But alas here we are. I am without you. Seasons pass and I am maturing and
    growing in wisdom and stature.
Thank you for instilling in me the values of love, joy, and acceptance, and
    for a golden childhood.

Be at peace father. I pray you find that deep serenity you so desperately sought.

May you find that joy in God's embrace.

Dad, I miss you. And when we meet we can laugh, dance, and sing together once more.

*Judah Chandra*

## Longing

What is this feeling inside, of disconnect and 'other'
This feeling of separation, from even mother and brother
Blocked from real touch, like a hand that is gloved;
Halting me from believing that I am unconditionally loved?

I sense such a loss, deep within my bones.
Yearning for connection, my whole spirit groans.
I look deep inside, and oh how so dark.
So hard to caress, my deep hurting heart.

Perhaps it is ego, or my unbridled pride
Inflated by fear and that tumult inside?
Perhaps it is trust in my own ability
Or my humour and charm masking true vulnerability?

Whatever it is, I long to be shown
Wherever I am, that I am not all alone.
In life's ups and downs, in all daily moans
To know I am loved. To know I am home.

*Judah Chandra*

## Compassion is a Bomber Jacket

Compassion is a bomber jacket
worn reversed.

People warm their hands
on fluff
and love you for the softness of the stuff.

Turn your jacket round,
put your own vessel first.

Let cold leather be your skin
then you can fly your plane
way up where air is sliver-thin
and warm yourself,
yourself,
as you guide
your solo mission in.

*Peter Chaplin*

## The Understudy

Every now and again
when the worship of the heaving crowd
and their violent adoration
becomes too loud,
as if to carry him off
overhead down the dusty street
and out of sight
to his own breast-beating funeral rite,
his foundation starts to crumble,
the eye liner starts to sting,
his costume pinches
and the brilliantly drawn character
lit up by ego and long scotches
in, frankly, dim and inadequate dressing rooms,
quakes,
the strain of constant excellence begins to tell,
the pain of leadership stoops
his broad Shakespearean frame,
his ears begin to ring,
his pulse booms,
some dark thing looms
that even whisky cannot quell.
Ladies and gentlemen,
the actor is unwell.

And so steps up a quieter man
to stand before the baying stalls.
Looks the same
if a little smaller, less made up,
less vain.
Plays the role a little more sober,
more contained, less pained.
Disappointing, doesn't have the balls,
the critics say.
And so the people stay away.

Yet some are drawn
by less clamour and less scorn.
They hear a subtler tone
perhaps more like their own.
And at the curtain
they don't set sail for local wine bars
protesting, short-changed,
noising their knowledgeable distaste,
but remain seated awhile
then gather in a loose, shy knot
at the stage door,
staying to thank the understudy
who told a tale they'd never heard before.

*Peter Chaplin*

## Burning Out

By rights a time of sleep,
arrive unbidden visitors
who rip to shreds
my flimsy veil of protection.
A maelstrom of nonsensical insistencies
worm inside my head.
Heart hammering
and sheet-tangles soaked
by the furnace of my skin,
my innards lurch to
a flailing sensation of
never-ending

        free

           fall . . .

Approaches the two-edged sword of dawn,
a threshold at once calming, (breathe),
yet portending the awful blade
of temporal existence.
Is this, finally, my day of defeat?
Or will I, with all my might, wring out
just one more blessed drop of willpower,
and, already spent,
push through to face
the hellholes of the day?

*Robert Davison*

## Hope

If darkness descends
and you see no way out,

If darkness weighs heavily
and your survival's in doubt,

If darkness overwhelms
and you simply give up,

I say softly, take comfort,
know that darkness
is transformation's midwife,
and that light will come
as surely as the dawn

*Robert Davison*

## Release

Aching to express
yet choosing
to depress
what's inside of me.

Is it unknowable,
or just unspeakable
trapped by the oughts of upbringing,
the fear of rejection or worse,
annihilation?
I swallow
and down it goes again,
compressed to a speck of dark matter.
into the swamp.

A lifetime's accumulation
wells up, then recedes,
wells up, then recedes,
threatening imminent havoc.

A turning.

Who is this half-expressed man
at once expansive and crushed?

A fledgling voice, cracked as an adolescent,
haltingly expresses a small truth,
and waits
for the sky to fall in.

Nothing.

The crisp air of freedom is intoxicating.
And behold,
the world is beautiful.

*Robert Davison*

# The Drumbeat of Falling

*For Andrew Smith*

First seen through smoke and drizzle,
a quiet, exotic presence. Sitting on a log.

Hours upon hours, sheltered in a wooden hut
shedding skin together, you left your woollen hat on.

Offering compassion and silent understanding,
we washed cups, waited and descended.

Depths were plumbed, scars revealed,
singing in a plain kitchen with other men.

Broken men – discovering gold
where shame and guilt lay buried.

Silence upon silence, eyes blurred by hot tears,
words telling only one part of the story.

You strengthened us, you bravely held us,
you blessed us, I believe you loved us.

Bonds forged through ritual, the drumbeat of falling.
Feeling your presence, lean and true.

The adamance of your heart shone through,
through doubts, through old wounds.

Unearthing the soulful soil, leaning on the spade, smiling.

Leaving a sacred space, creating new ones.

You left much too soon. For us.

*David Doyle*

## Choices

It's the lack of control,
That challenges most,
The, 'being forced to react'
Rather than, the 'choosing to respond'.

Despite our endless advancements, to 'infinity and beyond',
The primitive fears exist, lurking there,
In our reptilian brain,
Surfacing at every cough and sneeze.

United by anxiety, called to solidarity,
No borders now, empathy despite the isolation,
Smiles of re-assurance through the uncertainty and the distance,
Enforced stillness – giving us space.

How we fill it is up to us,
I hope we choose wisely.

*David Doyle*

## The Wounded Healer

Settled on the edge of the ancient plain
Where bog and forest once prevailed
The wounded healer creates an inland harbour
For those returning from stormy seas
Tempests of the heart and battered souls
The broken arrive one by one, and one by one are welcomed in.

Revealing his own wounds, still fresh despite remote origin
Like a modern Chiron – teaching, leading, sharing
Pierced by a poisoned arrow, still striding, stopping to serve
Bleeding love to those who appear, through dust and through tears
Holding the centre, sure footed on the ragged earth
The wisdom of love, transformed by a life

Allowing others the opportunity of transformation
Fiercely and gently.

*David Doyle*

## Returning to Love (what was never mine)

I first met you when I was a child
Acne scarred, longing for magic
We began the great journey together
Heart-strong and brave, emboldened by love
Looking towards each other, feeding the mystery
Renewing and relinquishing as best we could
Blessed beyond measure, through body, through soul, through love
Expanding the masterpiece twofold – through Ellen and Sam
Sweet, joy filled days of magnificent ordinariness
In love with love.

Then to be asked the impossible
Relinquishing all to love
Returning to love what was never mine
I never understood that love could ask so much

How can I trust love now – how do I remain true to love now
I vowed forever – in my beautiful naivety
Where to now? Now that you are gone.

*David Doyle*

*"And sometimes when the night is slow*
*the wretched and the meek*
*we gather up our hearts and go*
*a thousand kisses deep"*

L. Cohen

## Notice the Locks

I notice my competitive reflex again -
unconscious self-defence;
I'm better than you!
A locked-in reaction, armed and sharp, ready to outpace.
Does my yen to outsmart matter?
. . . Let it go. Loosen up.

Other days, when I walk into prison,
Clanking keys unlocking and locking gate after gate,
I run a time lapse movie in my mind, flower bud opening petal by petal.
I am here to contribute what I can, of grace, warmth, affirmation –
into a barred, bleak, brutal, shut-away-ness.

How to embrace the shadows?
Breathe, be present, smile welcome,
hold the space – expand the lungs – come fully into life . . . and love.

Sadness, anger, guilt, let it all flow away,
– release grief and tears to the ebbing current,
so the flood tide may wash back in, with that which heals.

What matters is generosity,
without a sense of superiority.
Be open, be positive, give and receive.
In this moment channel peace.

Consider how sunlight dawns, warms and enlivens.
Notice. Springtime buds break, blossom, then shatter and fade;
Next, seeds enrobe with flesh and swell into fruit.
Let flow this rich round of transformation.

Savour the changes, the cyclical nature of Creation;
renewal locked into each loop.
Out of the dirt, rain sparks us to bloom again,
. . . and again . . . and again.

Notice.

*Peter Fishpool*
*who volunteers as a Quaker*
*chaplain in a local prison*

## WeMen

WeMen crave closeness,
then back away;
afraid of losing
the false safety of separateness.

WeMen say we want affection,
but worry that might be weakness;
not believing we can ever be accepted
for who we really are.

WeMen want respect;
but by relying on domination
to affirm our fragile sense of ourselves,
we lose all hope of receiving it.

WeMen want love ;
desiring and reviling its wildness,
we can enter a woman's body
but won't let her into our soul.

*Steve Garrett*

## Fear

I often felt afraid
of being found out,
but really
I was just longing
to be found.

*Steve Garrett*

## The Spiral

Chiding my younger self
for his lack of understanding,
and regretting choices
that cannot be unmade,
is as foolish as an oak tree
reproaching an acorn
for not being bigger;
or a butterfly
blaming a caterpillar
for its lack of wings.
And when I open my heart and mind,
life is an expanding spiral,
revisiting but never repeating,
the ways I've been.

*Steve Garrett*

## Last Chance

In this mythical month of Sundays
I feel like an extra on the set
of a boring post apocalypse B-movie
that I can't walk away from.

In the city centre ragged humans cluster
with no-one to beg from;
the idea of social distancing a bad joke
to those who have always been given a wide berth

Families cramped in Council flats
are driving each other crazier than ever;
and men who use their fists to get silence or compliance
now have a truly captive audience.

But for those with Homes and Gardens
it's a welcomed paid break;
a chance for some family time.
Treats and meals delivered daily
while friends and family keep in contact
from a comfortable distance
Life is a walk in the park,
with cleaner air and more birdsong.

Drifting through these strangest of days
I marvel at how every rule of economics
can suddenly be broken with such impunity;
the official arguments for austerity
that left so many out in the cold
now revealed to be more like secrets and lies
than financial prudence.

Nature has pulled the rug out
from under our collective obsessions.
Which are now laid bare in their empty obesity.

The seemingly unstoppable train of consumption
has run out of steam
just before going over a cliff;
and we have time on our hands to wonder
if we really want to go back on board
or didn't realise until now
that we could get off and choose
a happier destination.

*Steve Garrett*

## All Change at The MOOT 2019

Setting off wrapped up warm and waterproofed
I step out of Dukes Barn, turning left,
taking my usual route.

Soon I'm met with road river running at me
eroding the asphalt
revealing the stones.
I step aside stomping along in my big boots.

Rainfall is returning down river to my right,
rushing, crashing, cascading over rocks
creating white frothy, foamy pools
as it heads seaward, recycling, to return again, recirculate.

Now I am stepping carefully on slippery, squelching mud,
risking humiliation at every step.
Newly planted saplings here in protective sleeves are
future trees, carbon dioxide convertors and trappers.

Suddenly I stop and stare.
I look in disbelief.
Ahead a shocking sight.
The woodland I know so well gone.
A muddy clearing with mechanical digger.
70-80 year old trees now stacks of tree trunks for timber.
No more a spot for me to rest and gaze at the river
With the sounds that flow from it.

'They're just a crop grown to harvest',
a local says as I return to Dukes Barn.
Forestry Commission farms the forests.
It's all change from a year ago
and so it is for me,
maybe not so drastic, devastating or apparent
but plenty more I cling to
in need of harvesting, recycling or clearing.

*Jonny Grant*

## A Last Wish

My father died at home in his bed.
A hidden undiagnosed cancer
left him holding a last wish to share
with his eldest grandson. Michael was
travelling to see him so here was
a chance for an unhurried goodbye.
A last chance to sit together as
Michael and Michael over a glass
of ale. This was no unplanned moment
but a concern to ease fears and place
dying at the heart of life's rhythms.
Supposedly there were three of us
in the room but I was stood down in
this closing chapter of a done life.
There to silently watch and witness.

Sitting on the bed alongside his
Grandfather it was unclear whether
Michael fully understood what was
about to take place. Very little
was said but what was said was spoken
in their silence as they rested in
the last of each others' company.
Michael opened the bottle of ale
pouring a first glass for his grandson
and a last glass for himself, his last.
Setting the empty bottle aside
he turned to face Michael and both their
glasses gently kissed softly – 'Sláinte'.
Nothing more was said but that they sat
in bonded silence. A right ending
to the modest way he lived his life.

A modest act imbued with feeling.
Perhaps a validation of the
ties between him and his grandson to
be remembered into the future.
Or simply, the ageless gesture of
an old man letting go. Yielding life
to his grandson and marking it with
an unspoken wisdom for all ages;
to bestow a place in his life's last
sacred moment, his last final wish.
Blessed benediction for someone
passing into manhood as he now
passes onto the next stage of life.
An experience for a young man
to hold and make of it what he will.

*Éamonn Kirke*

## What a Life

Fuck!
I am so pissed off.
Wandering down Dale Street
into Castle Street
I pass men and women of
all ages sleeping rough in
closed door ways and next to
soiled street furniture.
Sitting sprawled or slouched
in some drug alcohol
induced sanctuary.
What a life! What a price!

But then who am I to judge?
Who am I to stand back
and do nothing as if
it is nothing to do with me?
Who am I to give money yet
not look them in the eye,
avoiding all touch by dropping
surplus coins into crumpled cups?
I am relieved at how easy
money gives me a get out;
paying so as not to see,
paying so as not to feel.

What kind of people are we
that we can be unmoved
by this fucked up reality
as if there is no other way?
No other way robs us of all
heart-felt outrage and shame.
No other way simply means
no change and no chance!
The deeper truth of course
is that they are me and here in
Castle Street I am looking at
my own stone walls all pulled down.

I too am stranded alone
barely holding my own
in a thin life of show.
Wearily I hide my fears
from those too bored to care.
Wearily I walk the walk
paying a different price
for a life too much to bear.
Wearily I bind my pain
with delusions and distractions
stronger than cheap street booze;
paying so as not to weep.

*Éamonn Kirke*

## Today the World is United

Today the world is united in stillness.
Nothing has excited people as now.
Natural disasters, poverty, famine,
drought, injustice, genocide, war refugees,
all left us unmoved and untouched. Nothing
to lose sleep over or change our ways for.
The late-night news half heard over a
bottle of red wine rarely disturbed yet
nightly we listen in shock silence as a
virus tolls a death knell to our easy life.

It brings home the truth that in the end
we all die – a mystery we pretend
we can live without. Today the
world is united in that great unknown.
Faced with a nemesis that rips us from
make believe, we step back to secure
windows and doors till we are isolated
and alone in fear. Behind silent walls
what will we discover in our cells?
What will we remember about ourselves?

Today the world is united in terror
but do we respond in love or in fear?
Dreading what might be asked of us,
scared for who we might lose, we stumble. /
In desperation we cling to fear as
a comforting friend. A false prophet
offering false hopes that nothing will
change, that we are still in control.
Today our world is united in a wild
contagion of fear. It seems love has failed us.

A world built around love is a world without
borders or frontiers, a world where there is
enough for our needs and all are welcome. But,
a world built around fear and anxiety
demands exclusions and suspicions, begets
a sense of scarcity and suspends all hope.
In such a world voices of fear flourish,
in such a world we surrender ourselves
to easy certainties and lies. In such a world
we must practice love every day.

*Éamonn Kirke*

## A Life Unlived

My fear today is seeing
how small I have lived my life.
Saved in a box I almost
lived the life given to me.
Too late in life I leave this
box and to my surprise step
out on a lost road to me.
For too long I lived within
the fears of others failing
to see they were never mine.
So I nearly missed this life
simply living a quiet false
life never meant to be mine.
Now, it is all slowly changed
and I am not who I was.
Outside the box my life is
my own, my own mistakes, my
own fears, and I get to keep
to myself my hard won gains -
a life unlived by others.

*Éamonn Kirk*

# My Rites of Passage: Before, During and Hereafter

Dissembling
Frightening
Pretending
Controlling
Projecting
Resenting
Conflicting
Competing
Retreating
Avoiding
Fearing
Hurting
Stifling
Closing
Losing

Preparing
Drumming    Sharing
Listening        Opening
Giving              Releasing
Seeing                Feeling
Revealing          Receiving
Connecting      Facing
Healing    Sitting

*Neil Millar*

## Frames

Is that honey, or time
Dripping on my toast
As I make a snack
Because that's a thing
To do

Is that blood, or time
Dripping from my body
As a nosebleed
Alerts me
To the slow frantic panic
I'm feeling

Is that the world, or time
Seen through the frame
Of my window
Or my TV
As Lockdown
Which might go on for months
But has only been a few weeks
Moves slowly and emptily around

Reality, in this time
Lensed by events
Unforeseen
Because too busy
Doing nothing
To save the natural world
From fast actions
Of our species
Has now caught up
Having to pause

Get off the bus, the train
Delayed
Due to the wrong sort
Of virus on the line

And now, having the time
Or a big enough chunk
For a while
Long enough to perceive
My self
Reflected back
From absent routines
That might never return
If I am brave enough
To drop, like honey
On toast, slowly
Like blood dripping
My inside coming out
To be felt
And seen
And tasted
Anew

*Sandy McAfee*

## Mum and Me - our Last Day (on this earth at least)

I heard Benjamin Zephaniah say:
"Catch it whilst you can"

The time has come to stop asking questions
They demand too much

The time has come to sit and be
To trust we know how to be

When to say
What to do

And when to go
Expect: no more
My mum wants her body to go to Leeds Medical School

(When she's dead)

It'll no longer be mine either
I imagine watching
Inspecting for due reverence
I don't want my mum's limbs
Used in rag week

They'll need it quick
Student quacks have voracious appetites

So many gifts, right to the end

And beyond

*Richard Payne*

## Straitenings

*There is nothing I miss*
*No-one I need to hug*
*I'm enjoying the slowing down*
*The subtraction of complications*

Liminal space abounds
Excesses taped off as we return to source
And dive deep into the shadows of quarantine

Today we make our own myths
Of trips to Boots
And battles in Tesco

All we have harboured – cast adrift.
Horizons narrowed to new calibrations
Our focus re-attuned
On shores familiar and foreign

May we not emerge unscathed
But lithe to the possibilities
The storm creates

And for those that are lost
Here's hope our futures atone
As corrected courses pay honour
In ultimate communal salvation

*Richard Payne*

## A Pogonological Poem

My beard has got to a point where . . .

My wife can no longer restrain herself

A pocket mirror would be a strategic investment

People notice it

It casts its own shadow

It seems worthy of opinion

It may require attention

It may require investment

It seems more and more to be some kind of statement

It remains vulnerable

It retains significant moisture

It is some of the longest hair on my body

It receives offers I haven't received in years

It is becoming independent

I'm toying with shapes . . . and with colours!

It needs to be cut down to size

My wife has wondered aloud (and very much in my direction) whether it has "become a metaphor for me?"

I told my son I'd written a poem about my beard – he rolled his eyes at the word poem – he didn't stay for the beard part

I told my daughter I'd written a poem about my beard. "Would you like me to read it?" "No," she said, "but does it have the words weird and smeared in it?"

*Richard Payne*

## A Welcome Redemption

Our earliest welcomes are shot
Through family filters set
For and against the grain

How we were welcomed
Fixed in our fossil record
To be cracked open by curious, psycho geologist
On cheap day returns to our soul

They say there is a five second rule . . .
Look each other in the eye for five seconds and you will be drawn . . .

To kiss or kill

That's big picture stuff
A distraction from the hunt I am on
For what goes on in those first few primitive milliseconds?

Etched on our heart is the potted history of how we've been welcomed,
    treated and rejected

Relived every-time we look someone in the eye

I was heralded as a girl by my dad and sister – feminine names at the ready
Only my mum was steadfast to my gender
She knew what was brewing

On arrival I was a nuisance and a pest to all – finally harmony!
I arrived to a family that had run out of time – that had moved out and
    beyond.

I adopted being a nuisance and a pest believing it served me well.

"I'll show you awkward and I'll know that I can really trust those that see through; that come through for me."

Enough of you, my brothers, have now done that.

And now I get to wear my awkwardnesses in a different way – as a queer badge of honour and a beacon of weird hope

Yet traces of earlier attachment DNA linger in the afterlife
And I ask: "how strong the glow?"

Of my welcome

Of others

*Richard Payne*

## Discovering my Inner Child (2018) Or . . .

'SCHOOL PHOTOGRAPH RECOVERED': (Perry II 1965 OHS Shropshire)

ARE YOU A STRANGER WITHOUT EVEN A NAME

ENCLOSED AND FORGOTTEN BEHIND SOME OLD GLASS PANE?*

I find you, drawer stuffed, *Curled up*. The long photo recoils to
Hide your misery. Hidden too, the censored letters home. Hard Brush

flattened, a ten year old's *floating* hair, 'neath Regimented Rows

OF NAMES – A LOFTY SCOWLING BROTHER – PERRY I

– UNREACHABLE 'TWIXT RANKS ABOVE

Cross X legged, spirit hunched, empty eyed, hands clenched. Thrown
in the deep end, Perry (II) swims naked, frozen-feelinged, pulled into

a whirlpool shame of naked exposure

until my forever curling ruminations

again and again

find

*You*

*Mark Perry*

*courtesy of Eric Bogle: 'the Green Fields of France'

*After Calligrammes: Poems of Peace and War 1913-1916, by Guillaume
Apollinaire (1880 - 1918). Calligrammes are noted for how the typeface and
arrangement of the words play as much of a role in the meaning of each poem
as the words themselves – the form is called a calligra.*

## Gaining Stripes – Getting Stuck

"Six of the Best"
The cane left deeper stripes than three of the plimsole
    or my own leather slipper.
From six the fear set in. Stopped up my tears.
Whacker Worthington and Five Rivers' fingernails engraved us
    with long red weals of bitterness,
– Making their marks on us - As we forgot how to cry.

"He'll grow out of it"
Wet pyjamas left stinging red creases, as I hauled soaked sheets
    from the barred iron bed to the parade of bath tubs.
– More marks in us – As we forgot how to cry.

"We'll talk about that later"
Many tears of dried semen descend the aluminium walls.
– Walled off. I stuff someone else's girl back behind the cistern.

More marks in us, as we forgot . . .

*Mark Perry*

## Gift – from the Island

Mum, you left at 14, to board in Jamaica
Homesick and jealous, the only sibling not to return

Now I flannel wipe your fallen body
Unseen near sixty years
One side all black and blue
Crumpled and sad
I wind you like a baby

There's a glint on your wrist still
You remind me of your mother's bangle – you had asked her for it
But returning from the island
Your younger sister wore it

Seeing your hurt
Dad got it copied
'He really wanted me to have it'
'It's better than the real one'
Its golden arms embracing your thin wrist

Your mother always said: 'He's too clever by half'
That's not all, I think
Maybe that's how the healing starts?
'Mum – what about a foot rub?'

*Mark Perry*


*This is about my mum (90): a bedside poem written just before I had to institutionalise her in a care home. She first left her island at 3 with Polio, then at 10-11 with another sickness, that became homesickness. Boarding was part of colonial life.*

## waking naked

I sleep naked,
begin my day that way,
and am glad to shed my
layers as I return.

We all began that way,
naked from the womb, and
take nothing with us as we go,
except perhaps the memories
of how this changing body
has been loved and celebrated
as a baby first of all,
then all grown up.

I sleep naked.
It reminds me
that I am a sexual being,
sufficient, satient and hungry,
vulnerable, centred and questioning.

We drink in intimacy.
we crave touch,
and as babies recognise
our skin is a receptor
to the world.

I have slept naked
for so long
I can no longer find memory
of childhood pyjamas,
only of memorising
the spelling!
and the smooth touch on my face
of a pale-green "eiderdown"
as it snuggled around me.

In those pre-duvet days
I always would wonder
why I could not sleep there
directly beneath it,
having it hug me,
not tidied away under
tightly tucked-in sheet
and woollen blanket.

Mostly I remember
being in the bath,
and sliding on the bottom
when it drained.

A bath takes longer, running
it hot as you can manage
while you're in it,
sinking beneath its heat
in womb-like comfort.

These days I take longer
in the shower,
with unknown words
from deep inside
to pray aloud
and put the world
to rights, and breathe
a long sigh, and
let all its troubles drop off me.

Warmed, damp and naked,
I find perspective,
and often that's where
I find the words to write.

It's skin we understand:
our changing body that we live in.
*Touch, expensive as it is,*
*is all-important.*
The first clothes, they say:
the skin and fur of other creatures,
warmth against the cold.
Skin is constantly replaced.
Technically, it's not the same skin
that we're in.  It heals
and regenerates, but retains
memory.  Scars and blemishes
tell stories that remain
our continuity.
We must love the skin we're in.

For as long as I have it
I'll retain the habit
of settling into my own skin.
When I'm ready for sleep,
I am glad to shed my layers.
I sleep naked.

*Andy Raine*

## Saint Obvious the Unexpected

Obvious never expected to be a saint,
obviously.  No-one had ever paid
much attention to Obvious,  except
close friends,  and complicated
relatives. ( Each of them had an
It's Complicated story!)  Obvious
just muddled through everyday
life,  and wondered whether it
was usual to have so many
detours,  calamities and disappointments,
to know disaster well enough
to pick up a conversation
from when they last sat together.

One day, Obvious met Numinous
for  coffee,  quite by chance,  of course.
Numinous the Surprising.
"Can I have a hug?"  said Numinous.
What, here?  thought Obvious,
(not wanting to be conspicuous)
but said,  instead,  "Of course".
So Obvious embraced Numinous,
obviously,  right there in the coffee-shop.
Then they sat down.

"I needed that," said Numinous,
"and you're good to hug because
you've been in so many scrapes
you've no rough edges left,
and no sharp words, no cutting
corners . . ."
"That's surprising," said Obvious,
and smiled. "More coffee?"

So Numinous, welcomed by Obvious,
didn't hurry away, but sat right there,
and could soon be seen
with soft breath blowing, cooling the surface
of the hot coffee,
and enjoying conversation with a friend.

*Andy Raine*

## MANifesto

I am a man. I live. I breathe. I hunger.
I thirst.
I am a man. My body tells me I am a child no longer.
But often I behave like a boy even now, walking in the body of a man.
I am slow to turn my energies to caring for others: I care about myself.
I want to be loved. I crave affirmation.
I am a man. I want to make my mark upon the world.
I want to live, and I want my life to have meaning.
Now I am strong. Now I am secure.
I put to one side the need to just please myself.
I am a man, a sexual being, with physicality and desire.
I live with that hunger each day. I am a man, a boy no longer.
I am a man – and certainly not a woman!
I am a man, and more than just an animal. I learn from life.
I can work hard. I understand sacrifice.
I like to be liked. I love to belong,
but also I can stand alone.

*Andy Raine*

## Inspire

Let go of this insisting
you must have something to say.
When the well is dry,
let it be dry

Notice the chalky dust there
watch it rise under
the heat of attention,
revealing the sun's slanting light

Now visible, the void's
currents creep
a lazy dance in space
unencumbered by intention

unconcerned by 'next'
or 'new', progress, purpose
or hell's great warrior
'Significance'

The altogether empty lung,
she will feast on the incoming tide
Now give, now take. Let run, reel in.
exhale, inhale, expire, inspire

*Simon Ray*

## Black light

Life is fast, is ever new
A nature show time-lapse.
Flowers grow in seconds
And twitching carcasses rot
in painted light

Or we are old and slow
Deep stones in the pebbled stream
holding place like tired truths
touched by so much water
reinventing, babbling ten thousand tongues

I turn back to visit a familiar grief
check the stones marking the ground
And find the scene utterly changed
Green and gold given way
Folded in to rich blacks

All here is turned, encrypted layers
Rotting griefs and fresh fallen loves

Under this stone
One old bulb braves new growth
carbon deposits alight in fibreoptic shoots
Heralding still richer blacks, dynamic range,
And next season's colour

*Simon Ray*

## Where I stand (Turangawaewae)

Where will I take my stand?
What will it be like?

What will the ground be like?
Is the terrain uneven? Rocky?
Is there tussock grass and gorse?
Can I see trees?

Is there a smell? Earth and turning leaves, salt hints?
Is the air moving. Can I feel it on my face, between my fingers?
Do I hear, overhead, birds?

What stand
Will I take?
Any. Here I am.
ready to stand.

*Simon Ray*

## Blank Page

I wish I could fill this blank page
With the most beautiful poem,
But my mind is numb and fickle
No stories worth recalling through the years.

Everything seems told and retold in circles
Like a broken record scratched and old,
I don't want to go there anymore
Digging out the grime and sorrow

From murky ponds of darkness clogged with humus.
There's nothing moving anymore,
Dried ink in a frozen pen,
No looking back or projecting forward,

The now, torn asunder on a wasted page
To paradoxical to grasp;
Nothing as bad as a blank page
The lost words safe in sanctuary towers,

Or entombed in granite boulders,
I have no will to toil at its hard face.
I'll wait here, for the wind and the rain
To release them, from their frozen prism

*David Richardson*

## Rusty Doors

We talked until the celestial night
Grew tired and red eyed
Until the mid-night hour
Descended like a warm blanket
On a worn-out end of day.

The last curls of wispy smoke
Drifted high into the tall trees
A ceiling canopy of rustling leaves
Illuminating the gathering darkness
With glowing embers of a circled fire.

We revealed our sacred stories honestly
To all the listeners, silent attentive gaze
Told of broken promises, our vows of youth
Of ships that sailed on memories tide
Of denying wounds with blind pride.

Rusty doors, reluctantly prised open
And can never again, be closed.

*David Richardson*

## Ode to My Trade

I was reminded just recently
In a very nostalgic conversation,
That once upon a former lifetime
I was, a Sheet Metal Worker by trade.
Well to give it its grand old title
I was a Journeyman Sheet Metal Worker.
Journeyman, A title dating back to the 16<sup>th</sup> century;

I kept my old union card as a keepsake,
A souvenir of my initiation ritual.
A journey from apprentice, to trades-man.
It lies buried now in a bottom drawer
With the other bric-a-brac that we gather,
Faded, like the memories that visit sometimes,
When the wind changes its course
Blowing in ghosts, who recall the old stories.

It seems they don't give trades grand titles anymore
Everything is cut short, like an abbreviation.
A master craftsman of woodwork is slandered a chippy,
Creative seamstress, worker of magic weaves
Is reduced to the rag-trade,
Somehow diminishing the skills of the artisan.

In this throwaway world of mass production
Learn your trade well, with enthusiasm and time.

*David Richardson*

## The Long Windows

A blue coffee cup stands,
Faded, on the bleached windowsill,
Discarded, among expired magazines,
A year or so old,

Sets of ring-stains
Mark like Olympic symbols.
The finishing line in sight,
For these crooked people
In their marathon of life.

They gather as stiff as sticks
Anxiously resting along the walls
Worrying, worrying, worrying,
A virus of death at the door
Their loved ones banished from sight,
They are as lonely as the lost.

Outside the long windows
The falling leaves lament.
Soft eyes almost liquid
Telling their own story
Terrified to speak the truth,

I am afraid.

*David Richardson*

# Empire to Earth Pilgrim

## Empire

The crowded cacophony of Bangkok
Mean and miserable faces
Seem strange and unforgiving
Hurrying towards the next chemical cake or caffeine fix
The traffic is suffocating
The noise overwhelming
I disappear in the Seven Eleven glare
Manufactured food and manufactured lives
The smell of effluent seeps from the sidewalks
The many dogs sleep in the coolness of the doorways
The crushing towers loom over me
My breath is sucked into concrete and glass
Business and buying and buyout
How empty the transactions
Costing the Earth
Costing the Soul
What does it profit me if I gain the whole world but lose my soul?
What does it profit me if I gain the whole world but lose my soul?
What does it profit me if I gain the whole world but lose my soul?
Money makes the world go round and round and round ...
Dizziness in the then and the there
Concrete
A frog jumps in
Statue

**Earth Pilgrim**

The roosters open wide the day
The dogs answer the call
The pigs announce themselves too
The daughters gather and gabble
The mothers cook rice and fish
The fathers farm the land
Generations upon generations have come and gone
Leading the way through the dark forest
Reality is not measured out in paper
Brothers and Sisters, Aunts and Uncles
Bring us security, sanity and treasury
Rooted and grounded in heredity
Sharing identity, born in adversity
Striving humanity, from the depths of time
Life is found in the living,
Born in the cycles of giving and forgiving
Is this how we can prosper when we lose the world but gain our soul?
Is this how we can prosper when we lose the world but gain our soul?
Is this how we can prosper when we lose the world but gain our soul?
Partners make the world go round and round and round ….
Happiness in the here and the now
Rain
A frog laughs
The Earth sings!

*Francis Rothery*

## The Man Who Broke into Prison

Curious that a man
Breaks into prison.
Empty prison.
Seeking
to experience what?

Years of pain left here
Regrets of a wasted life,
Should have walked away.

Despair, hopelessness,
powerlessness contained
and imprisoned here.
Did he find anger, injustice
and demons of aggression?

Were lives saved here
as they hit the bottom,
was there prayer in this place?

Was there compassion, kindness
or brotherhood?
Creativity the saviour.

Or did he discover that
We all break into a prison
Of our own making.

*Peter Sadler*

*Based on a story that appeared on Youtube.*

## Second Chance

I have been here before
though people say it is strange and weird.
An initiate, in a novitiate,
One walk per week.
An initiation to a new life,
A new me.

Then I couldn't let go of the old,
Even now I can't let go.

For all of us, this is a second chance,
Take it.
Let go, fall down,
Come to life.

Sooner or later we will face what we used to call demons,
Anxiety, stress, and fear.
After we will certainly leave the cave.
This is the way of the world
– always a second chance.

*Peter Sadler*

## Bread of Life

Who are you that these people
should eat you up?
Watch yourself disappear
until you say "Where am I?"
or "Who am I?"

Will who you are not, teach you
who you really are,

I am not shame
not fear
not failure
not guilt.

I know all these
but I am love
I am peace.

*Peter Sadler*

## Morning Tide

Urgent restless, relentlessness,
tormented pulling.
No-going-back energy crashes.
Surging, sweeping.

No reflection, no mirror,
No energy in me,
Only a sad sea.

Watch, allow.
Sea calling me,
"Wake up, you are alive!"

As the sea energy finds me,
Lulls me to life,
Finds me, loves me,
Brings me home,
Sea in my body.

*Peter Sadler*

## A Man Cracking Open

*(how men become safer around women)*

There is a moment in a male life
when the mirror that he's used
to paint his image onto his face
smashes.

First the image distorts
and when he looks at it, he is no
longer sure who it is that looks
back.

Then it begins to revolve
each day, twisting and turning,
revealing faces, he never knew he
possessed.

He sees his Father in the
wrinkle at the corner of his eye and his
Mother in the blocked and bloody
tear-duct.

Then the long and inescapable
lament starts down in his spleen,
as the shadows in cast-off faces
gather.

There is blood somewhere
lurking in that mirror, hot and viscous
and sooner or later, it shows itself, it
flows.

And then we are back to that day
when the mirror smashes, it may go all
at once or it may take a few really hefty
blows.

The shock and the silence after
that splintering is like a diagnosis, it
opens up all the ignored places, it
lacerates.

    If he has any of the sense he was born
with he will enter the cave of his wounds
and not seek to run, this is a place that is a
fatality.

    The one thing the smashed mirror
reveals is that he does not know the way out,
he does not know what to do apart from a
myth.

    That half-remembered dream of a
leviathan that swallowed and carried him,
like a dark womb, and the only requirement -
surrender.

    And after such time as is needed
the beast will disgorge him, and he will find
that he has such tender wounds and a new
horizon.

    Then he will, if he can face the
excruciating sensation of skin after scabs,
encounter others and recognise that these too
are men cracked open.

Postscript: to any women reading – after all this he still has work to do.

*Adrian Scott*

## A Moment in each Day

*There is a Moment in each Day that Satan cannot find . . .*
William Blake

There is such a dirtiness around the outside of the house
at this time of year, everywhere is filthy. Where does all
this muddiness come from? I think it must be all the leaves
that autumn left behind itself like an untidy teenager.

It's outfits discarded, scattered until this February rain
turns them to a porridge of dark slurry that sticks
to the feet of my dogs. It happens when I obey the yelps
and open the door to their need for freedom from winter.

I have been grilling myself every day now, questioning
myself fiercely about the end of things; the end of mid-life;
the last vestiges of adolescence sticking to my children;
the end of my old dog's life who died last September as
the leaves began to separate and flutter, and his chest stilled.

There has been so much rain this year, the deluged
snowdrops who are usually like tiny huddles
of umpires conferring, white heads matching the white frost
are now more like a clump of fans at a washed-out football match
left standing bedraggled and debating when to leave.

And of course, the rain is because it is so inordinately warm
and the daffodils too early, are shouting their yellowness
into a dirty world that is nowhere near ready for spring.

And now I'm out with the young dog, as the night has drawn out
a little and I catch sight of that ground floor maisonette window,
with the empty love seat in front of it and the woman staring
out as she washes up a plate, then a cup in her mid-fifties.
The heating flu is belching out fog clouding the evening,
as she wipes the final teaspoon, putting it in the plastic pot
on the draining board, and her eyes have pooled endlessness.

Looking past me, past the dog, up the road past the blue sign
of the coop, into the muddying sky. Her gaze makes me turn
to see the white vapour trail of an aeroplane searing through
the growing darkness heading, neither of us knows where.

Infinity is a place to her, a refuge that she seeks out
when the need for reverie is greater than the sum of all
the parts of her life that don't add up to something good
and the mud in mine is so clogging I can't slough it off.

*Adrian Scott*

## John Speddings – Steel Worker
## 1947 - 2017

*Ten thousand long days I have rang you,*
*And all for untimely old age*

Joseph Senior – Smithy Rhymes and Stithy Chimes

The face he sets to the world
falls short of the man he used to be,
and yet the steel he worked
is still visible, assayed and tensile,
in his stainless-steel stare.

The Drop Forge's dirty process,
has filled his lungs,
by shifts; earlies, lates and nights,
with the slack and slough,
the searing breath of the furnace.

We sit in his living room.
His dark mahogany tea in our workmen's mugs,
as we look at his photograph of the 'black hole of Calcutta'
that was Turton-Platts' River Don Works,
looking like an old master in satanic oils.

*'It were great'*, he tells me
*'when we were Sheffield owned,*
*but we ended up, bought and sold, in the hands*
*of Australians and then the Yanks'*;
this man's fate sealed in Sydney or Pittsburgh.

Four men, mates, worked the forge,
gauging with precision the moment
when the great concussion would
press out another cherry red buffer
that would slowly harden into brazen steel
and keep the trains apart from each other.

Some men died, three during his service,
*'it's dangerous stuff, steel-working'*, he says
in the deadpan nonchalance of his ilk,
*'but you should have seen us,*
*leavin' works, black as the ace of spades,*
*muscled, I lost three stone when I were an apprentice'.*

He has been a buffer too, between
the life of steel forged, hammered into his frame,
the constancy of dropping,
casting his life to its contours,
and his family shielded from it all
sitting around his Woodhouse table.

The heat has withdrawn and
the workshops have fallen silent.
His body is Sheffield's, this is our body,
all of us the inheritors of his labour
but he is succumbing to his wounds.

This listening, a taking in,
an absorption of a face, a form,
a man uncertain now in the city he built,
cocks of London Road no more,
the city centre – an alien world not visited.

What honours do his kind receive?
When is his medal ceremony?
The life he gave is unnoticed,
except by me in this drinking of tea,
and by his family, by his friends,
and it's not enough, not nearly enough.

*Adrian Scott*

## Knights and Rites

The Looking Glass
You must stay with the pain of a simple, cleft heart
Let it smash to the ground or else pierce like a dart;
The mirror's hard surface, all chipped, black and red
Holds the key to the mystery your soul is not dead.

Ash
Clothe yourselves, then, my brothers, with ash, grey as dust
Here a humble reminder on earth that things rust;
Take away the tough lesson that all must decay
Before God lifts you up on your Resurrection Day.

The Room of Mourning
I have entered the castle of darkness at last
And awakened the dragon of fear at men's blast;
Their loud cries of anger, of sorrow and pain
Open up deep within me old wounds that still reign.

The Wilderness Charge
Go embrace, now, your demons or else set them free
In the wilderness journey, keep a note of your dreams;
Let glen springs refresh you, drink deep from that source
Where God waits to anoint you and 'Awaken the Force.'

In the Glen
As I sit watching water, the wind from above
Whispers to me, so gently: 'Come wash now, my Love;
Lay down all your burdens, let truth set you free
Become grafted to God's vine, you live now in me.'

Last Rites
Rites of passage completed the challenge remains:
Spend your bags of gold wisely, live in service, renamed;
Return home from the Bield reconciled, healed, made new
You're no longer a savage, but men Faithful and True.

*Andrew Sully*

## A Note on Knights and Rites

When I did my Rites in 2016, the children's school hymn, 'When a Knight won his Spurs', was for some reason like an earworm in my head. Maybe it had something to do with a sense of being on a  sacred quest and journey ; maybe too the Knight archetype celebrated in that hymn: gentle and brave, gallant and bold, riding for God and for valour through the land; facing the threats posed by  (inner) demons: the giants, dragons and ogres of 'storyland'. The three versed hymn ends:

*Let faith be my shield and let joy be my stead*
*'Gainst the dragons of anger the ogres of greed;*
*And let me set free with the sword of my youth*
*From the castle of darkness the power of the truth.*

During the rites I found myself writing several verses to the same metre of my earworm hymn, trying to retain the hymn's child-like innocence and simple, unsophisticated vocabulary and rhyme scheme.

*Andrew Sully*

## One Evening

One evening I sat on the ground with my father
I saw the delicate curve of his spine
That held the weight of thought
For so many years
Perhaps it was the years of bowing to the gods of work that shaped him so

That evening
He in his bedclothes
And me in mine
I looked at the way his body folded
With tender awkwardness
How young he looked out of a suit

I could see
His hands
His feet in particular
And thought
You were once a child

What were you like?

Did you throw stones through the windows of old ruins?
And feel the ecstasy
Of the glass breaking
And in that sound
Feel as if another part of you had just broken open

Did you build a den in the woods?
Your own wild kingdom
A place where your imagination could breathe and be itself
Did you hold your own hand in the dark when you were frightened?
Did you kill an animal?
What did you dream of?

Did that place in you
That place only you know
But no one else knows
Hidden from the world
That place
Just behind the heart
In the dark red cave of warm flesh

Did you feel a piercing love reach you there?
Just there
I hope so father
I hope so

*Cai Tomos*